I KNOW THE SCRIPTURES ARE TRUE

Elaine Cannon
Illustrated by Tara Larsen Chang

Bookcraft
Salt Lake City, Utah

1998 Primary Theme

All scripture is given by inspiration of God, and is profitable.

—2 Timothy 3:16

Copyright © 1997 by Elaine Cannon

All rights reserved. No part of this book may be reproduced in any form or by any means for commercial purposes without permission in writing from the publisher, Bookcraft, Inc., 1848 West 2300 South, Salt Lake City, Utah 84119.

Bookcraft is a registered trademark of Bookcraft, Inc.

ISBN 1-57008-341-X

First Printing, 1997

Printed in the United States of America

Every day, television and radio stations report bad news, but that doesn't mean there isn't any good news. There's lots of good news, and it teaches me how to be happy and wise and become more like our beloved Savior, Jesus Christ.

Whhen I read and study the scriptures of The Church of Jesus Christ of Latter-day Saints, I find lots of good news. The Holy Bible contains the Old and New Testaments. The Book of Mormon is another testament of Jesus Christ.

The Doctrine and Covenants contains revelations given to Joseph Smith and other modern-day prophets. The Pearl of Great Price contains revelations, translations, and narrations of the Prophet Joseph Smith.

Even though I am still a little child and can't read everything in the standard works, I know the scriptures are true!

I asked Heavenly Father if the scriptures are true, and he answered my prayers. The Holy Spirit tells me that the messages in the scriptures come from God. They are for our good!

M y Primary teacher tells me that Heavenly Father and Jesus want us to go back and live with them someday. The scriptures teach me how to do this.

HOW?

The scriptures teach me that if I do what is right I will be happier. They teach me not to be frightened when I get sick or lost or disappointed. They teach me to love and forgive even when someone is unkind to me.

The scriptures teach me so many important values, like:

Do not steal. (See Mosiah 13:22.)
Love one another. (See John 13:34.)
Keep the Sabbath day holy. (See Exodus 20:8.)

Serve others. (See Matthew 25:40.)
Walk in the ways of truth. (See Mosiah 4:15.)
Obey your parents. (See Ephesians 6:1.)

All the Prophets of God have said that the scriptures are true.

Nephi said, "My soul delighteth in the scriptures, and my heart pondereth them, . . . for the learning and the profit of my children" (2 Nephi 4:15).

Isaiah said, "Seek ye out of the book of the Lord, and read" (Isaiah 34:16).

Joseph Smith said, "I told the brethren that the Book of Mormon was the most correct of any book on earth, and the keystone of our religion" (The Teachings of Joseph Smith, [Bookcraft: Salt Lake City, 1997], p. 87).

President Gordon B. Hinckley said, "We know that the Book of Mormon is a true testament of the reality and divinity of the Lord Jesus Christ" (Ensign, October 1996, p. 5).

Paul said, "For whatsoever things were written aforetime were written for our learning, that we through patience and comfort of the scriptures might have hope" (Romans 15:4).

John, the Revelator, said, "Blessed is he that readeth, and they that hear the words of this prophecy, and keep those things which are written therein" (Revelation 1:3).

The Lord Jesus Christ says the scriptures are true. He said, "Search these commandments, for they are true and faithful, and the prophecies and promises which are in them shall all be fulfilled" (D&C 1:37). I believe Jesus.

As I learn and live as the scriptures say, I will become more and more like Jesus! Someday I can be encircled in the arms of his love. And that is the good news!

One day it may be said of me, "From a child thou hast known the holy scriptures, which are able to make thee wise unto salvation through faith which is in Christ Jesus" (2 Timothy 3:15).